GOD'S
VIBES MATTER DEVOTIONAL
A 30-Day Journey of Renewing Your Mind and Embracing This Season

JULIANA PAGE

BALBOA PRESS
A DIVISION OF HAY HOUSE

Copyright © 2018 Juliana Page.

All rights reserved. No part of this book may be used or reproduced by any means, graphic, electronic, or mechanical, including photocopying, recording, taping or by any information storage retrieval system without the written permission of the author except in the case of brief quotations embodied in critical articles and reviews.

This book is a work of non-fiction. Unless otherwise noted, the author and the publisher make no explicit guarantees as to the accuracy of the information contained in this book and in some cases, names of people and places have been altered to protect their privacy.

Balboa Press books may be ordered through booksellers or by contacting:

Balboa Press
A Division of Hay House
1663 Liberty Drive
Bloomington, IN 47403
www.balboapress.com
1 (877) 407-4847

Because of the dynamic nature of the Internet, any web addresses or links contained in this book may have changed since publication and may no longer be valid. The views expressed in this work are solely those of the author and do not necessarily reflect the views of the publisher, and the publisher hereby disclaims any responsibility for them.

The author of this book does not dispense medical advice or prescribe the use of any technique as a form of treatment for physical, emotional, or medical problems without the advice of a physician, either directly or indirectly. The intent of the author is only to offer information of a general nature to help you in your quest for emotional and spiritual well-being. In the event you use any of the information in this book for yourself, which is your constitutional right, the author and the publisher assume no responsibility for your actions.

Any people depicted in stock imagery provided by Getty Images are models, and such images are being used for illustrative purposes only. Certain stock imagery © Getty Images.

Print information available on the last page.

ISBN: 978-1-9822-0646-8 (sc)
ISBN: 978-1-9822-0670-3 (e)

Balboa Press rev. date: 06/15/2018

Contents

About The Author vii
Introduction ix
About The Devotional xi

Devotional

Template 1
Scripture References 35

About The Author

Recognized as a life-changing speaker and a prophetic voice for the next generation, Juliana Page's mission is to encourage and equip men and women from around the world to walk in their God-given purpose and fulfill destiny.

As a dynamic reformer and author, Page challenges people to break generational patterns and rise above societal pressures.

Page delivers life-giving strategies, eternal wisdom and an unwavering devotion to help you live your most authentic, joyful and significant life.

Her authentic and relatable approach has enabled people from all walks of life to discover spiritual solutions to earthly struggles and walk worthy of their unique callings.

Introduction

How is it that some of us see challenges and flee, while others see challenges and press in? This reaction versus response approach may have something to do with what we've cultivated in our minds. Fortunately, God has designed us in his image and likeness and he's designed us to grow and evolve in our maturity in him. This means that we can start where we are, and partner with the Holy Spirit to renew our minds and cultivate God's approach to our lives.

Whether you'd consider yourself a novice or a seasoned follower of Christ, all of us are given the daily opportunity to begin again with God—to renew our minds through the power of his Spirit, grow and stretch in our experience of him and embrace the season he has given us. This God's Vibes Matter devotional is designed to encourage you to fix your eyes on Jesus and to be still and know God. No other source will do. Our answers are not in the universe, in the stars or through practicing the laws of attraction. Our devotion is set on Christ and we keep it set.

Right believing holds the power to change your life. Consider what you've been cultivating in the garden of your soul. Is it pointing you back to the cross? Are you resisting the season you're planted in because you want something different? What is God telling you? His wonderful new is before you. He's waiting to meet with you. Begin again.

About The Devotional

My friend, this 30-day daily devotional is an invitation and a challenge for you that I believe will change your life! Over the next 30 days, I'd like for you to explore greater intimacy with God. God wants you whole. He wants you to live with the peace that surpasses all understanding and an unshakeable confidence in what he has done for you. Too often we live life in resistance and we miss out on the fullness of the season we're in because we've yielded to wrong thinking and believing which results in defeat, guilt, fears and addictions. Trials come when we allow the busyness, stressors and distractions of life to overwhelm us and draw us away from what we know to be true.

Sometimes God infiltrates our cozy Christianity with his unconventional methods so that we can emerge better for it. When you make a bold decision to set your mind to believe in God's love for you, you will let go of the life of heaviness and defeat and pursue your divine destiny full of victory, security and success. No matter what challenges you face, God is a precise God with perfect timing. Just like you would find encouragement and renewed perspective from a coach, invite Jesus to an intimate chat with you. Meet with God with an expectant heart and allow God's Word to refresh and reshape your thinking, speaking and decision making.

As you begin, reflect on the season you're in. This is merely an exercise to assist you in proactively partnering with God. Once you have a sense of the season you're in, let the scripture references and daily devotional provide a context of how Jesus, your coach, might inspire and encourage you where you are. I've noticed that the Holy Spirit tends to show up in many ways and often when you least expect him, so be open to new ways of hearing his voice and sensing his presence. All I ask is that over the next 30 days you set aside 15-30 minutes with the Lord to discover what season he has you positioned in and how he wants you to discover personal restoration and revival where you are.

Here is a breakdown of how God helped me to grow in greater intimacy with him and how you might approach this book.

1. God is your coach! God is a champion in your absence and a friend always. In other words, no matter how many times you may neglect or run from God, he has never wavered in his love for you. He delights in you and enjoys spending time with you just like you would experience with your best friend. If you can view God as all his wonderful names, but particularly during this devotional as your greatest counselor, guide or coach, this allows you to come boldly to him with your questions, cares and hearts desires. He's always ready to meet with you.

    "For a child will be born to us, a son will be given to us; And the government will rest on His shoulders; And His name will be called Wonderful Counselor, Mighty God, Eternal Father, Prince of Peace" (*New American Standard*, Isaiah 9:6).

2. There is a time and season for everything. Discerning the voice of God is a divine mystery because it is the supernatural work the Holy Spirit does in us. There is no formula that gives us 100 percent accuracy in hearing from God, but growing in wisdom and discernment is something that we can ask God for and it is something we can practice and mature in. We tend to struggle when we compare our season to someone else's, when we resist where we are or when we become frustrated because we can't see God working in our circumstances. God is always working whether we are aware of it or not. We all can grow in our capacity to work our seasons with all diligence rather than resisting them. God started his mighty work in you and he is faithful to complete it. Will you be content in encounters with him and fully convinced of his goodness or will you frustrate the grace he's given?

    "To every thing there is a season, and a time to every purpose under the heaven: A time to be born, and a time to die; a time to plant, and a time to pluck up that which is planted; A time to kill, and a time to heal; a time to break down, and a time to build up; A time to weep, and a time to laugh; a time to mourn, and a time to dance; A time to cast away stones, and a time to gather stones together; a time to embrace, and a time to refrain from embracing; A time to get, and a time to lose; a time to keep, and a time to cast away; A time to rend, and a time to sew; a time to keep silence, and a time to speak; A time to love, and a time to hate; a time of war, and a time of peace" (*King James Version*, Ecclesiastes 3:1-8).

Reflect on the season God may have you in right now. This exercise will support your process of being fully present where God has you. While we may often find ourselves sowing in every season, there are also times that are primarily about preparing us for the next level in God or maturing what we've learned. For example, if you are in a season of development, it wouldn't be healthy to expect a harvest. If you can discern your season, you won't be tempted to run out ahead of God or get overwhelmed in the waiting. Here are some examples of seasons:

Sowing-a season of development in one of more areas of your life. We can't expect a harvest if we are not planting any seeds. This is a season where you are intentional about what and where you are sowing because you've received glimpses through your eyes of faith of what God's promised.

Growing-a season of maturing and preparing for what's to come. Sometimes we think we're ready for so much more than our character and soul capacity can manage. This is a season of tests and trials to bring to light where your faith is, where you have room to grow and how you can deepen your experience with God.

Blossoming-a season of breakthrough into a new level, anointing or intimacy with God. We love hearing messages about victory and elevation, but when it comes, we can't be trying to get prepared, we must be ready to act. An example of this could be when a someone seemingly out of nowhere and no way emerges from an unknown lifestyle to a public platform. The elevation is not as instant as it seems and often reflects years of sowing and growing. In a season of elevation, it is important to maintain the character and integrity that keep you strong and steady in God and ready to move at a moment's notice.

3. Pray always! Prayer is one of the best ways to open your heart completely to what the Holy Spirit wants to teach you and the way he wants to teach it. In our own understanding we are limited in our knowledge of God's character and his purposes. As we embrace opportunities to process with him and pray through what we're facing, we become greater receivers of who God is and what God has for us. For the next

30 days, set your mind on your relationship with the Lord. Invite God into your life using the *PRAY* model to heighten your spiritual senses.

"This is the confidence that we have in approaching God: that if we ask anything according to his will, he hears us" (*New International Version*, 1 John 5:14).

P   **PRAISE**

Take the first moments before the Lord and praise him for who he is. As you praise God you will enter his presence and you will shift your focus off the things of this world that occupy your attention.

R   **REPENT**

Picture a foggy glass of water. This represents that sin in thought, word or deed that can prevent you from being a clear glass fit for the Master's use. If there is anything weighing on you that you are being led to repent of, take some time to do this sincerely and allow the Lord to cleanse and purify you.

A   **ASK**

God's Word reveals that we shall have what we say and often the things that we don't have are due to us not asking for them. What would you ask the Lord for if you knew he would answer exceedingly abundantly beyond what you could ask or imagine?

Y   **YIELD**

Yielding is acting as if God has given you your "yes" already. Yield to the Holy Spirit and do not lean on your own understanding, get caught up in distractions or waver. If you've asked for what is promised in His Word, His Word shall not return void. Act in faith as you wait.

Be still and listen to what God is saying to you in his garden of truth. Let his words of grace saturate your spirit as you meditate on each one. Day by day, he will break the chains of faulty thinking and realign you with his vision and promises for you. This is God's promise to his children, "The LORD will guide you always; he will satisfy your needs in a sun-scorched land and will strengthen your frame. You will be like a well-watered garden, like a spring whose waters never fail" (*New International Version*, Isaiah 58:11).

Get ready for a greater revelation of God's grace toward you, and the power of his finished work in your life that will transform you from the inside out. It's time to embrace your season!

DEVOTIONAL

"But Seek Ye First the kingdom of God, and his righteousness and all these things shall be added unto you"

(Matthew 6:33, KJV)

TEMPLATE

DAY 1

PRAISE

Remember Who God is! Who does His Word say that he is? Write it here.

"God, I praise you for your wonderful works. Your goodness and mercy are beyond my comprehension. I thank you that you never leave me and you never forsake me. I praise you for adopting me and being my ever-present help. I praise you for your love and divine orchestration that leave me in constant awe of you. I praise you for your light. In you there is no darkness at all."

REPENT

What do you need to release that is hindering your connection with God?
What cares are you carrying that God desires to carry?
What is God teaching you to trust him with?
What do you know to be true (confirmed by God's Word) versus what you feel?

Release	Cares to Cast	I Trust You With
Distractions- i.e.-my time on social media	Resisting my work circumstances versus working wholeheartedly unto God	My life-Isaiah 42: 6-8, NIV

Gossip- witnessing others talk about someone or speaking about others when they are not present	Offenses and opinions of others. God is the only judge. My job it to forgive.	My finances-Phil. 4:19, KJV
Murmuring- speaking fears or complaints rather than prophesying truth and encouragement	My future-worrying about rather than trusting how things will come together	My future-Jer. 29:11, NKJV
Unhealthy Relationships-anyone that is disrespecting my boundaries or leading me away from God	Family/Friends- considering what they are walking through more than the power of God	My relationships- Eph. 4:2-3, NIV

ASK

Ask God for what you have need of according to his Word. Take a scripture from his good news to you and declare it over your life as your answer to whatever you are facing.

Scripture Verse:
"Consider the lilies how they grow: they toil not, they spin not; and yet I say unto you, that Solomon in all his glory was not arrayed like one of these" (*King James Version*, Luke 12:27).

YIELD

Take what God has revealed to you in your devotional time and receive it with a heart full of gratitude. Turn what you've learned into a prayer of thanksgiving to your heavenly Father.

"Thank you, Father, for reminding me that you are in control and for giving me this metaphor of the lilies and how they grow. I repent that I have been resisting you and questioning circumstances in my life. By your strength, show up strong in my weaknesses. Help me to trust in you with all my heart. Be my confidence and guide my steps because of my enemies. I yield to you."

God's Vibes Matter Devotional

Day 1 Date: _____

Praise
Remember Who God is! Who does his Word say that he is? Write it here.
_____
_____
_____
_____

Repent
What do you need to release that is hindering your connection with God?
What cares are you carrying that God desires to carry?
What is God teaching you to trust him with?
What do you know to be true (confirmed by God's Word) versus what you feel?

Release	Cares to Cast	I Trust You With

Ask
Ask God for what you have need of according to his Word. Take a scripture from his good news to you and declare it over your life as your answer to whatever you are facing.

Scripture Verse:
_____
_____

Yield
Take what God has revealed to you in your devotional time and receive it with a heart full of gratitude. Turn what you've learned into a prayer of thanksgiving to your heavenly Father.

Revelation:
_____
_____
_____

Juliana Page

Day 2 Date: _____

Praise

Remember Who God is! Who does his Word say that he is? Write it here.

_____
_____
_____
_____

Repent

What do you need to release that is hindering your connection with God?
What cares are you carrying that God desires to carry?
What is God teaching you to trust him with?
What do you know to be true (confirmed by God's Word) versus what you feel?

Release	Cares to Cast	I Trust You With

Ask

Ask God for what you have need of according to his Word. Take a scripture from his good news to you and declare it over your life as your answer to whatever you are facing.

Scripture Verse:

_____
_____

Yield

Take what God has revealed to you in your devotional time and receive it with a heart full of gratitude. Turn what you've learned into a prayer of thanksgiving to your heavenly Father.

Revelation:

_____
_____
_____

God's Vibes Matter Devotional

Day 3 Date: _____

Praise
Remember Who God is! Who does his Word say that he is? Write it here.

_____
_____
_____
_____

Repent
What do you need to release that is hindering your connection with God?
What cares are you carrying that God desires to carry?
What is God teaching you to trust him with?
What do you know to be true (confirmed by God's Word) versus what you feel?

Release	Cares to Cast	I Trust You With

Ask
Ask God for what you have need of according to his Word. Take a scripture from his good news to you and declare it over your life as your answer to whatever you are facing.

Scripture Verse: _____
_____

Yield
Take what God has revealed to you in your devotional time and receive it with a heart full of gratitude. Turn what you've learned into a prayer of thanksgiving to your heavenly Father.

Revelation: _____
_____
_____

Juliana Page

Day 4 Date: _____

Praise
Remember Who God is! Who does his Word say that he is? Write it here.
_____
_____
_____
_____

Repent
What do you need to release that is hindering your connection with God?
What cares are you carrying that God desires to carry?
What is God teaching you to trust him with?
What do you know to be true (confirmed by God's Word) versus what you feel?

Release	Cares to Cast	I Trust You With

Ask
Ask God for what you have need of according to his Word. Take a scripture from his good news to you and declare it over your life as your answer to whatever you are facing.

Scripture Verse:
_____
_____

Yield
Take what God has revealed to you in your devotional time and receive it with a heart full of gratitude. Turn what you've learned into a prayer of thanksgiving to your heavenly Father.

Revelation:
_____
_____
_____

Day 5 Date: _____

Praise
Remember Who God is! Who does his Word say that he is? Write it here.
_____
_____
_____
_____

Repent
What do you need to release that is hindering your connection with God?
What cares are you carrying that God desires to carry?
What is God teaching you to trust him with?
What do you know to be true (confirmed by God's Word) versus what you feel?

Release	Cares to Cast	I Trust You With

Ask
Ask God for what you have need of according to his Word. Take a scripture from his good news to you and declare it over your life as your answer to whatever you are facing.

Scripture Verse:
_____
_____

Yield
Take what God has revealed to you in your devotional time and receive it with a heart full of gratitude. Turn what you've learned into a prayer of thanksgiving to your heavenly Father.

Revelation:
_____
_____
_____

Day 6 Date: _____

Praise
Remember Who God is! Who does his Word say that he is? Write it here.
_____
_____
_____
_____

Repent
What do you need to release that is hindering your connection with God?
What cares are you carrying that God desires to carry?
What is God teaching you to trust him with?
What do you know to be true (confirmed by God's Word) versus what you feel?

Release	Cares to Cast	I Trust You With

Ask
Ask God for what you have need of according to his Word. Take a scripture from his good news to you and declare it over your life as your answer to whatever you are facing.

Scripture Verse:
_____
_____

Yield
Take what God has revealed to you in your devotional time and receive it with a heart full of gratitude. Turn what you've learned into a prayer of thanksgiving to your heavenly Father.

Revelation:
_____
_____
_____

God's Vibes Matter Devotional

Day 7 Date: _____

Praise
Remember Who God is! Who does his Word say that he is? Write it here.
_____
_____
_____
_____

Repent
What do you need to release that is hindering your connection with God?
What cares are you carrying that God desires to carry?
What is God teaching you to trust him with?
What do you know to be true (confirmed by God's Word) versus what you feel?

Release	Cares to Cast	I Trust You With

Ask
Ask God for what you have need of according to his Word. Take a scripture from his good news to you and declare it over your life as your answer to whatever you are facing.

Scripture Verse:
_____
_____

Yield
Take what God has revealed to you in your devotional time and receive it with a heart full of gratitude. Turn what you've learned into a prayer of thanksgiving to your heavenly Father.

Revelation:
_____
_____
_____

Juliana Page

Day 8 Date: _____

Praise
Remember Who God is! Who does his Word say that he is? Write it here.
_____
_____
_____

Repent
What do you need to release that is hindering your connection with God?
What cares are you carrying that God desires to carry?
What is God teaching you to trust him with?
What do you know to be true (confirmed by God's Word) versus what you feel?

Release	Cares to Cast	I Trust You With

Ask
Ask God for what you have need of according to his Word. Take a scripture from his good news to you and declare it over your life as your answer to whatever you are facing.

Scripture Verse:
_____
_____

Yield
Take what God has revealed to you in your devotional time and receive it with a heart full of gratitude. Turn what you've learned into a prayer of thanksgiving to your heavenly Father.

Revelation:
_____
_____
_____

Day 9 Date: _____

Praise
Remember Who God is! Who does his Word say that he is? Write it here.

_____
_____
_____
_____

Repent
What do you need to release that is hindering your connection with God?
What cares are you carrying that God desires to carry?
What is God teaching you to trust him with?
What do you know to be true (confirmed by God's Word) versus what you feel?

Release	Cares to Cast	I Trust You With

Ask
Ask God for what you have need of according to his Word. Take a scripture from his good news to you and declare it over your life as your answer to whatever you are facing.

Scripture Verse:

_____
_____

Yield
Take what God has revealed to you in your devotional time and receive it with a heart full of gratitude. Turn what you've learned into a prayer of thanksgiving to your heavenly Father.

Revelation:

_____
_____
_____

Juliana Page

Day 10 Date: _____

Praise

Remember Who God is! Who does his Word say that he is? Write it here.

_____
_____
_____
_____

Repent

What do you need to release that is hindering your connection with God?
What cares are you carrying that God desires to carry?
What is God teaching you to trust him with?
What do you know to be true (confirmed by God's Word) versus what you feel?

Release	Cares to Cast	I Trust You With

Ask

Ask God for what you have need of according to his Word. Take a scripture from his good news to you and declare it over your life as your answer to whatever you are facing.

Scripture Verse:

_____
_____

Yield

Take what God has revealed to you in your devotional time and receive it with a heart full of gratitude. Turn what you've learned into a prayer of thanksgiving to your heavenly Father.

Revelation:

_____
_____
_____

Day 11 Date: _____

Praise
Remember Who God is! Who does his Word say that he is? Write it here.
_____
_____
_____
_____

Repent
What do you need to release that is hindering your connection with God?
What cares are you carrying that God desires to carry?
What is God teaching you to trust him with?
What do you know to be true (confirmed by God's Word) versus what you feel?

Release	Cares to Cast	I Trust You With

Ask
Ask God for what you have need of according to his Word. Take a scripture from his good news to you and declare it over your life as your answer to whatever you are facing.

Scripture Verse:
_____
_____

Yield
Take what God has revealed to you in your devotional time and receive it with a heart full of gratitude. Turn what you've learned into a prayer of thanksgiving to your heavenly Father.

Revelation:
_____
_____
_____

Juliana Page

Day 12 Date: _____

Praise
Remember Who God is! Who does his Word say that he is? Write it here.
_____
_____
_____
_____

Repent
What do you need to release that is hindering your connection with God?
What cares are you carrying that God desires to carry?
What is God teaching you to trust him with?
What do you know to be true (confirmed by God's Word) versus what you feel?

Release	Cares to Cast	I Trust You With

Ask
Ask God for what you have need of according to his Word. Take a scripture from his good news to you and declare it over your life as your answer to whatever you are facing.

Scripture Verse:
_____
_____

Yield
Take what God has revealed to you in your devotional time and receive it with a heart full of gratitude. Turn what you've learned into a prayer of thanksgiving to your heavenly Father.

Revelation:
_____
_____
_____

God's Vibes Matter Devotional

Day 13 Date: _____

Praise
Remember Who God is! Who does his Word say that he is? Write it here.
_____
_____
_____
_____

Repent
What do you need to release that is hindering your connection with God?
What cares are you carrying that God desires to carry?
What is God teaching you to trust him with?
What do you know to be true (confirmed by God's Word) versus what you feel?

Release	Cares to Cast	I Trust You With

Ask
Ask God for what you have need of according to his Word. Take a scripture from his good news to you and declare it over your life as your answer to whatever you are facing.

Scripture Verse:
_____
_____

Yield
Take what God has revealed to you in your devotional time and receive it with a heart full of gratitude. Turn what you've learned into a prayer of thanksgiving to your heavenly Father.

Revelation:
_____
_____
_____

Juliana Page

Day 14 Date: _____

Praise

Remember Who God is! Who does his Word say that he is? Write it here.

_____
_____
_____

Repent

What do you need to release that is hindering your connection with God?
What cares are you carrying that God desires to carry?
What is God teaching you to trust him with?
What do you know to be true (confirmed by God's Word) versus what you feel?

Release	Cares to Cast	I Trust You With

Ask

Ask God for what you have need of according to his Word. Take a scripture from his good news to you and declare it over your life as your answer to whatever you are facing.

Scripture Verse:

_____
_____

Yield

Take what God has revealed to you in your devotional time and receive it with a heart full of gratitude. Turn what you've learned into a prayer of thanksgiving to your heavenly Father.

Revelation:

_____
_____
_____

God's Vibes Matter Devotional

Day 15 Date: _____

Praise
Remember Who God is! Who does his Word say that he is? Write it here.

_____
_____
_____
_____

Repent
What do you need to release that is hindering your connection with God?
What cares are you carrying that God desires to carry?
What is God teaching you to trust him with?
What do you know to be true (confirmed by God's Word) versus what you feel?

Release	Cares to Cast	I Trust You With

Ask
Ask God for what you have need of according to his Word. Take a scripture from his good news to you and declare it over your life as your answer to whatever you are facing.

Scripture Verse: _____
_____

Yield
Take what God has revealed to you in your devotional time and receive it with a heart full of gratitude. Turn what you've learned into a prayer of thanksgiving to your heavenly Father.

Revelation: _____
_____
_____

Juliana Page

Day 16 Date: _____

Praise
Remember Who God is! Who does his Word say that he is? Write it here.
_____
_____
_____
_____

Repent
What do you need to release that is hindering your connection with God?
What cares are you carrying that God desires to carry?
What is God teaching you to trust him with?
What do you know to be true (confirmed by God's Word) versus what you feel?

Release	Cares to Cast	I Trust You With

Ask
Ask God for what you have need of according to his Word. Take a scripture from his good news to you and declare it over your life as your answer to whatever you are facing.

Scripture Verse:
_____
_____

Yield
Take what God has revealed to you in your devotional time and receive it with a heart full of gratitude. Turn what you've learned into a prayer of thanksgiving to your heavenly Father.

Revelation:
_____
_____
_____

God's Vibes Matter Devotional

Day 17 Date: _____

Praise
Remember Who God is! Who does his Word say that he is? Write it here.
_____
_____
_____
_____

Repent
What do you need to release that is hindering your connection with God?
What cares are you carrying that God desires to carry?
What is God teaching you to trust him with?
What do you know to be true (confirmed by God's Word) versus what you feel?

Release	Cares to Cast	I Trust You With

Ask
Ask God for what you have need of according to his Word. Take a scripture from his good news to you and declare it over your life as your answer to whatever you are facing.

Scripture Verse:
_____
_____

Yield
Take what God has revealed to you in your devotional time and receive it with a heart full of gratitude. Turn what you've learned into a prayer of thanksgiving to your heavenly Father.

Revelation:
_____
_____

Day 18 Date: _____

Praise
Remember Who God is! Who does his Word say that he is? Write it here.
_____
_____
_____
_____

Repent
What do you need to release that is hindering your connection with God?
What cares are you carrying that God desires to carry?
What is God teaching you to trust him with?
What do you know to be true (confirmed by God's Word) versus what you feel?

Release	Cares to Cast	I Trust You With

Ask
Ask God for what you have need of according to his Word. Take a scripture from his good news to you and declare it over your life as your answer to whatever you are facing.

Scripture Verse:
_____
_____

Yield
Take what God has revealed to you in your devotional time and receive it with a heart full of gratitude. Turn what you've learned into a prayer of thanksgiving to your heavenly Father.

Revelation:
_____
_____
_____

Day 19 Date: _____

Praise
Remember Who God is! Who does his Word say that he is? Write it here.

_____
_____
_____
_____

Repent
What do you need to release that is hindering your connection with God?
What cares are you carrying that God desires to carry?
What is God teaching you to trust him with?
What do you know to be true (confirmed by God's Word) versus what you feel?

Release	Cares to Cast	I Trust You With

Ask
Ask God for what you have need of according to his Word. Take a scripture from his good news to you and declare it over your life as your answer to whatever you are facing.

Scripture Verse:
_____
_____

Yield
Take what God has revealed to you in your devotional time and receive it with a heart full of gratitude. Turn what you've learned into a prayer of thanksgiving to your heavenly Father.

Revelation:
_____
_____
_____

Juliana Page

Day 20 Date: _____

Praise
Remember Who God is! Who does his Word say that he is? Write it here.
_____
_____
_____

Repent
What do you need to release that is hindering your connection with God?
What cares are you carrying that God desires to carry?
What is God teaching you to trust him with?
What do you know to be true (confirmed by God's Word) versus what you feel?

Release	Cares to Cast	I Trust You With

Ask
Ask God for what you have need of according to his Word. Take a scripture from his good news to you and declare it over your life as your answer to whatever you are facing.

Scripture Verse:
_____
_____

Yield
Take what God has revealed to you in your devotional time and receive it with a heart full of gratitude. Turn what you've learned into a prayer of thanksgiving to your heavenly Father.

Revelation:
_____
_____
_____

Day 21 Date: _____

Praise
Remember Who God is! Who does his Word say that he is? Write it here.
_____
_____
_____
_____

Repent
What do you need to release that is hindering your connection with God?
What cares are you carrying that God desires to carry?
What is God teaching you to trust him with?
What do you know to be true (confirmed by God's Word) versus what you feel?

Release	Cares to Cast	I Trust You With

Ask
Ask God for what you have need of according to his Word. Take a scripture from his good news to you and declare it over your life as your answer to whatever you are facing.

Scripture Verse:
_____
_____

Yield
Take what God has revealed to you in your devotional time and receive it with a heart full of gratitude. Turn what you've learned into a prayer of thanksgiving to your heavenly Father.

Revelation:
_____
_____
_____

Juliana Page

Day 22 Date: _____

Praise

Remember Who God is! Who does his Word say that he is? Write it here.

_____
_____
_____
_____

Repent

What do you need to release that is hindering your connection with God?
What cares are you carrying that God desires to carry?
What is God teaching you to trust him with?
What do you know to be true (confirmed by God's Word) versus what you feel?

Release	Cares to Cast	I Trust You With

Ask

Ask God for what you have need of according to his Word. Take a scripture from his good news to you and declare it over your life as your answer to whatever you are facing.

Scripture Verse:

_____
_____

Yield

Take what God has revealed to you in your devotional time and receive it with a heart full of gratitude. Turn what you've learned into a prayer of thanksgiving to your heavenly Father.

Revelation:

_____
_____
_____

God's Vibes Matter Devotional

Day 23 Date: _____

Praise
Remember Who God is! Who does his Word say that he is? Write it here.
_____
_____
_____
_____

Repent
What do you need to release that is hindering your connection with God?
What cares are you carrying that God desires to carry?
What is God teaching you to trust him with?
What do you know to be true (confirmed by God's Word) versus what you feel?

Release	Cares to Cast	I Trust You With

Ask
Ask God for what you have need of according to his Word. Take a scripture from his good news to you and declare it over your life as your answer to whatever you are facing.

Scripture Verse:
_____
_____

Yield
Take what God has revealed to you in your devotional time and receive it with a heart full of gratitude. Turn what you've learned into a prayer of thanksgiving to your heavenly Father.

Revelation:
_____
_____
_____

Juliana Page

Day 24 Date: _____

Praise

Remember Who God is! Who does his Word say that he is? Write it here.

_____
_____
_____
_____

Repent

What do you need to release that is hindering your connection with God?
What cares are you carrying that God desires to carry?
What is God teaching you to trust him with?
What do you know to be true (confirmed by God's Word) versus what you feel?

Release	Cares to Cast	I Trust You With

Ask

Ask God for what you have need of according to his Word. Take a scripture from his good news to you and declare it over your life as your answer to whatever you are facing.

Scripture Verse:

_____
_____

Yield

Take what God has revealed to you in your devotional time and receive it with a heart full of gratitude. Turn what you've learned into a prayer of thanksgiving to your heavenly Father.

Revelation:

_____
_____
_____

Day 25 Date: _____

Praise
Remember Who God is! Who does his Word say that he is? Write it here.
_____
_____
_____
_____

Repent
What do you need to release that is hindering your connection with God?
What cares are you carrying that God desires to carry?
What is God teaching you to trust him with?
What do you know to be true (confirmed by God's Word) versus what you feel?

Release	Cares to Cast	I Trust You With

Ask
Ask God for what you have need of according to his Word. Take a scripture from his good news to you and declare it over your life as your answer to whatever you are facing.

Scripture Verse:
_____
_____

Yield
Take what God has revealed to you in your devotional time and receive it with a heart full of gratitude. Turn what you've learned into a prayer of thanksgiving to your heavenly Father.

Revelation:
_____
_____
_____

Juliana Page

Day 26 Date: _____

Praise

Remember Who God is! Who does his Word say that he is? Write it here.

_____
_____
_____
_____

Repent

What do you need to release that is hindering your connection with God?
What cares are you carrying that God desires to carry?
What is God teaching you to trust him with?
What do you know to be true (confirmed by God's Word) versus what you feel?

Release	Cares to Cast	I Trust You With

Ask

Ask God for what you have need of according to his Word. Take a scripture from his good news to you and declare it over your life as your answer to whatever you are facing.

Scripture Verse:

_____
_____

Yield

Take what God has revealed to you in your devotional time and receive it with a heart full of gratitude. Turn what you've learned into a prayer of thanksgiving to your heavenly Father.

Revelation:

_____
_____
_____

Day 27 Date: _____

Praise
Remember Who God is! Who does his Word say that he is? Write it here.

_____
_____
_____
_____

Repent
What do you need to release that is hindering your connection with God?
What cares are you carrying that God desires to carry?
What is God teaching you to trust him with?
What do you know to be true (confirmed by God's Word) versus what you feel?

Release	Cares to Cast	I Trust You With

Ask
Ask God for what you have need of according to his Word. Take a scripture from his good news to you and declare it over your life as your answer to whatever you are facing.

Scripture Verse:
_____
_____

Yield
Take what God has revealed to you in your devotional time and receive it with a heart full of gratitude. Turn what you've learned into a prayer of thanksgiving to your heavenly Father.

Revelation:
_____
_____
_____

Juliana Page

Day 28 Date: _____

Praise
Remember Who God is! Who does his Word say that he is? Write it here.
_____
_____
_____
_____

Repent
What do you need to release that is hindering your connection with God?
What cares are you carrying that God desires to carry?
What is God teaching you to trust him with?
What do you know to be true (confirmed by God's Word) versus what you feel?

Release	Cares to Cast	I Trust You With

Ask
Ask God for what you have need of according to his Word. Take a scripture from his good news to you and declare it over your life as your answer to whatever you are facing.

Scripture Verse:
_____
_____

Yield
Take what God has revealed to you in your devotional time and receive it with a heart full of gratitude. Turn what you've learned into a prayer of thanksgiving to your heavenly Father.

Revelation:
_____
_____
_____

Day 29 Date: _____

Praise
Remember Who God is! Who does his Word say that he is? Write it here.
_____
_____
_____
_____

Repent
What do you need to release that is hindering your connection with God?
What cares are you carrying that God desires to carry?
What is God teaching you to trust him with?
What do you know to be true (confirmed by God's Word) versus what you feel?

Release	Cares to Cast	I Trust You With

Ask
Ask God for what you have need of according to his Word. Take a scripture from his good news to you and declare it over your life as your answer to whatever you are facing.

Scripture Verse:
_____
_____

Yield
Take what God has revealed to you in your devotional time and receive it with a heart full of gratitude. Turn what you've learned into a prayer of thanksgiving to your heavenly Father.

Revelation:
_____
_____
_____

Juliana Page

Day 30 Date: _____

Praise
Remember Who God is! Who does his Word say that he is? Write it here.
_____
_____
_____
_____

Repent
What do you need to release that is hindering your connection with God?
What cares are you carrying that God desires to carry?
What is God teaching you to trust him with?
What do you know to be true (confirmed by God's Word) versus what you feel?

Release	Cares to Cast	I Trust You With

Ask
Ask God for what you have need of according to his Word. Take a scripture from his good news to you and declare it over your life as your answer to whatever you are facing.

Scripture Verse:
_____
_____

Yield
Take what God has revealed to you in your devotional time and receive it with a heart full of gratitude. Turn what you've learned into a prayer of thanksgiving to your heavenly Father.

Revelation:
_____
_____
_____

God's Vibes Matter Devotional

SHARE WHAT YOU'VE LEARNED

Are there any consistent scriptures, lessons, or Holy Spirit nudges for you to put here?

_____
_____
_____
_____

What are your top 3 takeaways from the month?

_____
_____
_____
_____

How have these revelations and lessons changed you as a leader?

_____
_____
_____
_____

How will you serve others in sharing what you know?

_____
_____
_____
_____

What are your next faith steps?

_____
_____
_____
_____

Juliana Page

How will you speak your future? Write a prophetic prayer:

___

Scripture References

SOWING-

"So God created man in His *own* **image**; in the **image** of God He created him; male and female He created them" (Genesis 1:27, NKJV).

"Light is **sow**n for the righteous, And gladness for the upright in heart" (Psalm 97:11, NKJV)

"On the same day Jesus went out of the house and sat by the sea. And great multitudes were gathered together to Him, so that He got into a boat and sat; and the whole multitude stood on the shore. Then He spoke many things to them in parables, saying: "Behold, a sower went out to sow. And as he sowed, some *seed* fell by the wayside; and the birds came and devoured them. Some fell on stony places, where they did not have much earth; and they immediately sprang up because they had no depth of earth. But when the sun was up they were scorched, and because they had no root they withered away. And some fell among thorns, and the thorns sprang up and choked them. But others fell on good ground and yielded a crop: some a hundredfold, some sixty, some thirty. He who has ears to hear, let him hear" (Matthew 13:1-8, NKJV)!

"Therefore hear the parable of the sower: When anyone hears the word of the kingdom, and does not understand *it,* then the wicked *one* comes and snatches away what was sown in his heart. This is he who received seed by the wayside. But he who received the seed on stony places, this is he who hears the word and immediately receives it with joy; yet he has no root in himself, but endures only for a while. For when tribulation or persecution arises because of the word, immediately he stumbles. Now he who received seed among the thorns is he who hears the word, and the cares of this world and the deceitfulness of riches choke the word, and he becomes unfruitful. But he who received seed on the good ground is he who hears the word and understands *it,* who indeed bears fruit and produces: some a hundredfold, some sixty, some thirty" (Matthew 13:18-23, NKJV).

"Another parable He put forth to them, saying: "The kingdom of heaven is like a man who sowed good seed in his field; but while men slept, his enemy came and sowed tares among the wheat and went his way. But when the grain had sprouted and produced a crop, then the tares also appeared. So the servants of the owner came and said to him, 'Sir, did you not sow good seed in your field? How then does it have tares?' He said to them, 'An enemy has done this.' The servants said to him, 'Do you want us then to go and gather them up?' But he said, 'No, lest while you gather up the tares you also uproot the wheat with them. Let both grow together until the harvest, and at the time of harvest I will say to the reapers, "First gather together the tares and bind them in bundles to burn them, but gather the wheat into my barn" (Matthew 13:24-30, NKJV)

"Another parable He put forth to them, saying: "The kingdom of heaven is like a mustard seed, which a man took and sowed in his field, which indeed is the least of all the seeds; but when it is grown it is greater than the herbs and becomes a tree, so that the birds of the air come and nest in its branches" (Matthew 13:31-32, NKJV).

"He answered and said to them: "He who sows the good seed is the Son of Man. [38] The field is the world, the good seeds are the sons of the kingdom, but the tares are the sons of the wicked *one*. [39] The enemy who sowed them is the devil, the harvest is the end of the age, and the reapers are the angels. [40] Therefore as the tares are gathered and burned in the fire, so it will be at the end of this age. [41] The Son of Man will send out His angels, and they will gather out of His kingdom all things that offend, and those who practice lawlessness, [42] and will cast them into the furnace of fire. There will be wailing and gnashing of teeth. [43] Then the righteous will shine forth as the sun in the kingdom of their Father. He who has ears to hear, let him hear" (Matthew 13: 37-43, NKJV)!

"Looking unto Jesus, the author and finisher of *our* faith, who for the joy that was set before Him endured the cross, despising the shame, and has sat down at the right hand of the throne of God" (Hebrews 12:2, NKJV).

"But the **fruit** of the Spirit is love, joy, peace, longsuffering, kindness, goodness, faithfulness, gentleness, self-control. Against such there is no law" (Galatians 5:22-23, NKJV).

"Then God said, "Let the earth bring forth grass, the herb *that* yields seed, *and* the **fruit** tree *that* yields **fruit** according to its kind, whose seed *is* in itself, on the earth"; and it was so" (Genesis 1:11, NKJV).

GROWING-

"The Lord rewarded me according to my **righteousness**; According to the cleanness of my hands He has recompensed me" (2 Samuel 22:21, NKJV).

"Let no corrupt word proceed out of your **mouth**, but what is good for necessary edification, that it may impart grace to the hearers" (Ephesians 4:29, NKJV)

"I am the true vine, and My Father is the vinedresser. Every branch in Me that does not bear fruit He takes away; and every *branch* that bears fruit He prunes, that it may bear more fruit. You are already clean because of the word which I have spoken to you. Abide in Me, and I in you. As the branch cannot bear fruit of itself, unless it abides in the vine, neither can you, unless you abide in Me. "I am the vine, you *are* the branches. He who abides in Me, and I in him, bears much fruit; for without Me you can do nothing. If anyone does not abide in Me, he is cast out as a branch and is withered; and they gather them and throw *them* into the fire, and they are burned. If you abide in Me, and My words abide in you, you will ask what you desire, and it shall be done for you. By this My Father is glorified, that you bear much fruit; so you will be My disciples" (John 15:1-8, NKJV)

"You shall **love** the Lord your God with all your heart, with all your soul, and with all your strength" (Deuteronomy 6:5, NKJV).

"Finally, my brethren, be strong in the Lord and in the power of His might. Put on the whole armor of God, that you may be able to stand against the wiles of the devil. For we do not wrestle against flesh and blood, but against principalities, against powers, against the rulers of the darkness of this age, against spiritual *hosts* of wickedness in the heavenly *places*. Therefore take up the whole armor of God, that you may be able to withstand in the evil day, and having done all, to stand. Stand therefore, having girded your waist with truth, having put on the breastplate of righteousness, and having shod your feet with the preparation of the gospel of peace; above all, taking the shield of faith with which you will be able to quench all the fiery darts of the wicked one. And take the helmet of salvation, and the sword of the Spirit, which is the word of God; praying always with all prayer and supplication in the Spirit, being watchful to this end with all perseverance and supplication for all the saints— and for me, that utterance may be given to me, that I may open my mouth boldly to make known the mystery of the gospel, for which I am an ambassador in chains; that in it I may speak boldly, as I ought to speak" (Ephesians 6:10-20, NKJV).

"And whenever you stand praying, if you have anything against anyone, forgive him, that your Father in heaven may also forgive you your trespasses" (Mark 11:25, NKJV).

"**Trust** in the Lord with all your heart, And lean not on your own understanding; In all your ways acknowledge Him, And He shall direct your paths" (Proverbs 3:5-6, NKJV).

"The Lord *is* my strength and song, And He has become my salvation; He *is* my God, and I will **praise** Him; My father's God, and I will exalt Him" (Exodus 15:2, NKJV).

"Be strong and of good **courage**, do not fear nor be afraid of them; for the Lord your God, He *is* the One who goes with you. He will not leave you nor forsake you" (Deuteronomy 31:6, NKJV).

"And God gave Solomon wisdom and exceedingly great **understanding**, and largeness of heart like the sand on the seashore" (1 Kings 4:29, NKJV).

BLOSSOMING-

"And the Feast of Harvest, the firstfruits of your labors which you have sown in the field; and the Feast of Ingathering at the end of the year, when you have gathered in *the fruit of* your labors from the field" (Exodus 23:16, NKJV).

"That fiftieth year shall be a Jubilee to you; in it you shall neither sow nor reap what **grow**s of its own accord, nor gather *the grapes* of your untended vine" (Leviticus 25:11, NKJV).

"I will make you exceedingly **fruit**ful; and I will make nations of you, and kings shall come from you" (Genesis 17:6, NKJV).

"For thus says the Lord: "Behold, I will extend peace to her like a river, And the glory of the Gentiles like a flowing **stream**. Then you shall feed; On *her* sides shall you be carried, And be dandled on *her* knees" (Isaiah 66:12, NKJV).

"For I know the thoughts that I think toward you, says the Lord, thoughts of peace and not of evil, to give you a future and a hope" (Jeremiah 29:11, NKJV).

"Then the Lord your God will bring you to the land which your fathers possessed, and you shall possess it. He will **prosper** you and multiply you more than your fathers" (Deuteronomy 30:5, NKJV).

"This Book of the Law shall not depart from your mouth, but you shall meditate in it day and night, that you may observe to do according to all that is written in it. For then you will make your way **prosper**ous, and then you will have good success" (Joshua 1:8, NKJV).

"And keep the charge of the Lord your God: to walk in His ways, to keep His statutes, His commandments, His judgments, and His testimonies, as it is written in the Law of Moses, that you may **prosper** in all that you do and wherever you turn" (1 Kings 2:3, NKJV).

"And Joshua said to the people, "Sanctify yourselves, for tomorrow the Lord will do wonders among you" (Joshua 3:5, NKJV).

"Be diligent to present yourself approved to God, a worker who does not need to be ashamed, rightly dividing the word of truth" (2 Timothy 2:15, NKJV).

Printed in the USA
CPSIA information can be obtained
at www.ICGtesting.com
LVHW020951280124
770161LV00007B/625

9 781982 206468